A MILLION
LETTERS
TO WRITE

A MILLION LETTERS TO WRITE

Angelina Schreiber

Bibliografische Information der Deutschen Nationalbibliothek: Die Deutsche Nationalbibliothek verzeichnet diese Publikation in der Deutschen Nationalbibliografie; detaillierte bibliografische Daten sind im Internet über http://dnb.dnb.de abrufbar.

© 2024 Angelina Schreiber
Verlag: BoD · Books on Demand GmbH, In de Tarpen 42, 22848 Norderstedt
Druck: Libri Plureos GmbH, Friedensallee 273, 22763 Hamburg

ISBN: 978-3-7693-1709-1

To Rebecca & Franka
to a million more moments to live – together

to your
inner child

While making my bed,
I carefully placed every stuffed animal
in its rightful place,
except one.

The tiny dog I got when I was little
has been sleeping on the floor for weeks now,
and I don't mind.
I left him there,
and I wonder why.

He meant the world to me back then,
my everything,
the one I couldn't sleep without,
the one who held all my fears
and all my comfort in his tiny, worn seams.

Maybe I've grown past that time,
maybe I've grown past him.
Or maybe it's something else,
something quieter,
a distance I can't quite explain.

I don't know if I've moved on,
or if I've just learned
to carry what he once gave me
in a different way now—
somewhere inside,
where no one else can see.

I hope when I see my daughter with her father,
I hope something in me can heal too.

I live alone,
but not lonely—
surrounded by the quiet hum of my own world,
protecting my inner child
like a precious, untamed spark.

Here, there is peace,
not the kind that comes from silence,
but the kind that grows
from loving myself as I once wished to be loved.

I nurture the small, tender parts of me,
the ones that were once forgotten,
and let them bloom in the safety
of my own company.

I live alone,
in peace,
with love—
and it feels like coming home to myself.

In another lifetime,
my inner child would have been loved
the way they deserved—
held gently, spoken to softly,
shielded from the storms they didn't understand.

But in this lifetime,
it's my hands that cradle them,
my voice that whispers, *you are safe now.*
I am the love they waited for,
the home they never had.

In this lifetime,
by me,
they are finally seen,
finally heard,
finally loved.

MY LETTER:

Angelina Schreiber

M Y   L E T T E R :

A Million Letters to Write

Angelina Schreiber

Thank you for being my anchor
when the waves got too high,
for holding me steady
when life itself seemed unsure
if it wanted me here.

You fought for me in ways
I may never fully understand,
and your love became the light
that led me back to myself.

I know it's your first time on this earth,
and yet, somehow,
you've always known how to love me.
For that, and for everything,
thank you.

Every flower that blooms in my heart,
every bright, wild thing within me,
is there because of you.
Your kindness became my sunlight,
your encouragement, my rain.

You tended to me
when I was too small to understand,
when I was too fragile to stand on my own.
And now, I grow,
rooted in the love you gave me.

I am who I am
because you never stopped believing
in what I could become.

He didn't deserve you,
he never did.
The way he broke you,
the way he left you carrying the weight
of two lives alone—
it was never fair.

But he gave you me,
and for that, I'll always be grateful.

I see the cracks he left behind,
the scars you tried to hide.
But I also see your strength,
your unwavering love,
the way you gave me everything
even when you had nothing left.

I will heal you,
heal us,
because you deserve a love
as steady and as fierce
as the one you gave me.

MY LETTER :

Angelina Schreiber

MY LETTER:

A Million Letters to Write

I spent 22 years waiting
for you to call me.
You never did.
Now I realize the calls
were always there,
just in another person.

It was the way you showed up—
steady, kind, and quietly strong,
the way you saw me,
not as someone you had to care for,
but as someone you chose to love.

What we share isn't in our veins,
but in the moments only we understand—
a bond built in laughter, in trust,
in the unspoken knowing
that family is something you create.

It was never blood;
it was always you.

You healed a heart
you didn't break,
mended wounds
that weren't yours to tend.

You stepped into my life
without hesitation,
bringing light
where shadows used to linger.

I could not be more grateful
for the way you stayed,
for the love you gave so freely,
for making a house a home.

You didn't have to,
but you chose to—
and in that choice,
you gave me something
I'll treasure forever.

By heart,
we became something stronger,
a bond unshaken
by the absence of blood.

M Y   L E T T E R :

Angelina Schreiber

M Y L E T T E R :

We are home.
You slam the door,
we shout some more.
I break your things,
you spill my drinks.

We are home.
You never give me a hug,
but we jam together to Lovebug.
You are home.

I hug you,
you say you hate me.
We cry.

And now,
I will never be home again.
I will never hear you slamming the door,
shouting some more,
spilling the drinks,
or making me laugh at the mess.

I will never be a kid with you again,
never feel that wild, chaotic love
we never quite put into words.

You made my home home.

I see you.
Through the noise,
through the names they try to pin on you,
through the shadows of who they think you should be—
I see you.

I see the strength it takes
to stand tall in a world
that doesn't always understand,
the courage in your quiet rebellion,
the beauty in your truest self.

No matter what they say,
no matter what they believe,
you are more than enough.

And I am proud—
proud of who you are,
proud of who you're becoming,
proud to stand beside you,
to see you for everything you are
and everything they don't.

No matter how hard we fight,
no matter the words we've thrown,
you will always be the best part
of my childhood.

The laughter, the mischief,
the shared secrets and dreams—
they're etched into who I am,
a part of me I'll never let go.

Through the chaos,
you were my constant,
my partner in every adventure,
my first friend.

And even now,
no matter how far we go,
you'll always hold that place
in my heart.

Forever,
I want to be your protector,
your safe place,
the one who makes sure
you never have to face
what I've already seen.

Stay where the light is,
where innocence lives—
and I'll stand guard,
always.

M Y   L E T T E R :

Angelina Schreiber

MY LETTER:

A Million Letters to Write

to the place
you call
home

Exactly one year ago, I was forced to move out of the apartment and environment that were meant to be my forever home. It wrecked me, broke me, and mostly scared me. I was afraid that moving out would mean losing the warm and cozy feeling of a home. I live alone now. I eat alone now. I am my own company now. And guess what? It doesn't scare me anymore to be on my own. It feels right. It feels like home. This is your sign that being on your own is not scary, bad, or sad. *Being on your own means finding yourself, learning to love yourself, and caring about yourself.* It means being at home with yourself no matter where you live or with whom you live together. No matter where you are in the future, you will always be your own home.

This body is meant
for so much more than hate,
more than the sharp words
and cruel gazes
it has endured.

This body is made to be a home—
a sanctuary of love,
of warmth,
of belonging.

Home is where
I can love loudly,
where my laughter echoes
without apology,
and my tears are met
with open arms.

Home is where
I never have to stay quiet,
never have to shrink
to fit someone else's comfort.

It's the space
where my heart beats freely,
where every part of me is welcome,
seen,
and safe.

Home is not a place—
it's the freedom to be
unapologetically me.

Home is where the sunflowers can rest in light,
their golden heads bowing in quiet contentment,
no longer reaching,
no longer searching,
but simply being.

It's the place where warmth lingers,
where even the smallest seeds of hope
are nurtured and bloom.

Home is not just a place,
but a feeling—a soft glow,
a steady presence,
a safe haven where everything fragile
can grow strong again.

M Y   L E T T E R :

Angelina Schreiber

M Y L E T T E R :

The scary part about growing up
is that I loved you so much at 16
and forgot about your existence at 22.

In another universe I hope
we would finally be complete together.
In another universe I hope
we would finally be happy.
In another universe
you and I would be different.

Our love was like Friday the 13th.
While crossing roads with black cats,
it was meant to break through episodes
of anxiety attacks.
Darling, we were so unlucky,
I turned us into poetry.

Oh, how the love we carried along
turned out to be just like the lost city Atlantis.
It drowned.
People forgot about its existence
and it started to turn into a mystery
not to be explored.
But for me it was real,
every glimpse of it.

Parting ways, no one stays,
wishing it was just a phase.
Remembering Sunday's,
holidays, kisses on the crossways.
About these days, writing essays,
still wishing for an always.

I hope when you see my face everywhere,
I hope that you feel ashamed.

You kept running towards the storm,
no wonder we lost each other.

When you wake up in another lifetime,
I hope you meet yourself along the way
and I hope you make yourself suffer.
The way you did with me.

You never bought me sunflowers—
hell, you never even brought me yellow flowers.
You always picked the ones you liked,
the ones you thought were cute,
wrapped them up with a smile,
never noticing the empty feeling
they left behind.

I wanted sunflowers, bright and bold,
something that felt like warmth, like joy—
something that felt like you'd been listening,
like you'd taken a moment to see me
to know what might make me smile.

But I got what you loved,
what you thought was enough,
and I learned to find beauty
in holding onto the quiet ache of wanting more.

How could I ever change
my favorite color from yellow to green,
trade the brightness of hope for something
quieter, something that feels more like leaving.

How could I ever let someone this close again,
when the memory of your touch still lingers
like a shadow, when trust feels like a bridge
you taught me to fear crossing?

How could I ever not choose myself,
when choosing you left me so empty,
so lost in the spaces where your love should have been?

How could you ever do this to me—
take the light I gave you and leave me in the dark?

M Y   L E T T E R :

_____
_____
_____
_____
_____
_____
_____
_____
_____
_____
_____
_____
_____
_____
_____
_____
_____
_____
_____
_____
_____
_____
_____
_____
_____
_____
_____
_____
_____

Angelina Schreiber

MY LETTER :

*to the
feeling of
falling*

I am falling and I can't get up
I am falling into the small kisses you gave me,
each one a spark,
lighting a path I can't seem to leave.

I am falling and I can't get up,
caught in the memory of your hands,
the way they held me like something delicate,
like something worth keeping.

I am falling, deeper,
into the warmth of your laughter,
the quiet strength of your gaze—
and I don't want to get up.

Life sent me through a test,
through storms that tore at my edges,
through falls that left me bruised and aching.
Each trial shaped me,
prepared me for something I couldn't see.

And then, there was you.

Falling never felt sweeter.
With you, it wasn't a descent—
it was a release,
like the storms had only taught me
how to trust the wind.

Every stumble led me here,
to this moment,
to this love that makes the fall
feel like flying.

You made me fall in love
with writing happy poems again,
with lines that lift, that sing, that breathe,
as if joy itself were ink on the page,
as if hope had found a voice in my hands.

You made me remember
the beauty in gentle words,
in love that doesn't ache, but shines,
a warmth I forgot could be real.

You made me fall in love with you,
with the quiet happiness of being seen,
with the ease of laughter that feels like home—
and now every poem is a piece of you,
echoing softly, full of light.

It was in those small, quiet moments
that I felt something I hadn't in years:
rest.

For a fleeting second,
my soul put down its armor,
and I let myself breathe.
Because for once,
I didn't have to do it all alone.

M Y   L E T T E R :

Angelina Schreiber

M Y L E T T E R :

_____

_____

_____

_____

_____

_____

_____

_____

_____

_____

_____

_____

_____

_____

_____

_____

_____

_____

_____

_____

_____

_____

_____

_____

_____

_____

_____

_____

_____

I flipped to page 218
on a random Saturday night
and all that kept me u
that night was *you.*

I want a love that stops time,
stops the background music,
a love that challenges,
a love that just makes sense.

Your eyes are the poem
I never intended to write.
But the tip of my pen
started to draw pretty lines
between you and I
and all I ever wanted was
to drown in our existence forever.

I long for the peace you give me,
when the whole world around me breaks in chaos.

I was so scared the sun will never shine again.
So scared until you showed me the stars.

I stare at the big ice cream pot in front of us,
the way your spoon dives in with such delight,
your laugh spilling over like the whipped cream on top.
And in this moment,
I know—this will last forever.

How bizarre, though,
because I hate ice cream.
I hate its cold bite, its sticky sweetness,
but somehow,
sharing this with you feels like love.

Maybe it's not about the ice cream at all.
Maybe it's about you,
about the way you make the things I dislike
feel like they're worth it.
Forever tastes sweeter when it's with you.

M Y   L E T T E R :

_____

_____

_____

_____

_____

_____

_____

_____

_____

_____

_____

_____

_____

_____

_____

_____

_____

_____

_____

_____

_____

_____

_____

_____

_____

_____

_____

_____

_____

_____

_____

Angelina Schreiber

M Y   L E T T E R :

A Million Letters to Write

*to the first
person you
loved*

All I ever wanted was
to find home in a person.

Maybe my father was right,
people are meant to leave.

When you left,
my whole world shattered.
It felt like the air was too heavy,
like I didn't belong here anymore.
I didn't want to see,
didn't want to feel,
just wanted the ache to stop.

But time passed.
And slowly,
the pieces you broke
started to mend themselves.

The lesson you left behind,
though wrapped in pain,
lives endlessly in my heart:
The first person
I should ever think about
is myself.

Not you.
Not anyone else.
Just me—
the one who will never leave.

When you left this earth,
the world shifted,
and the flower field we used to play in
grew quiet.

The blooms seemed to bow,
the air held its breath,
as if even nature mourned your absence.

I never knew how much light you gave
until it was gone,
how much joy lived in the simple moments
until they became memories.

Now, the field is still beautiful,
but it carries your echo,
a reminder that some presences
are never truly replaceable.

You were the beginning of a story
I didn't know how to write,
but I wrote it anyway,
with trembling hands and open pages.

Loving you was like stepping into sunlight—
warm, blinding, and fleeting.
You were my first taste of something infinite,
even if it wasn't meant to last.

MY LETTER:

Angelina Schreiber

M Y   L E T T E R :

_____

_____

_____

_____

_____

_____

_____

_____

_____

_____

_____

_____

_____

_____

_____

_____

_____

_____

_____

_____

_____

_____

_____

_____

_____

_____

_____

Angelina Schreiber

Don't waste energy on people
that are meant to leave.

Think about the ones
that will stay and dance
with you in the rain,
never complaining about being cold.

Angelina Schreiber

With you,
life feels a little less chaotic
and a little more like
strawberry vanilla ice cream
with a cherry on top.

With you,
I can be a little sister
in a lifetime
of always being the big and strong one.

We were girls together—
growing, stumbling, learning,
crying when the world felt too heavy,
laughing when it felt like nothing could stop us.

We've lost each other
in the chaos of life,
in the ebb and flow of time.
But somehow,
we always find our way back,
like the universe refuses
to keep us apart.

You are far more than my best friend.
You are my constant,
my safe place,
my person—
the one who knows me
in ways even I don't fully understand.

No matter where life takes us,
you will always be home to me.

Sometimes, people just fit—
not in a way that can be explained,
but in the quiet understanding of their souls,
in the way their laughter feels like music
meant to be shared.

Sometimes, life works its quiet magic,
bringing two strangers together
from entirely different paths,
only to show them they were always
meant to meet.

And just like that,
they fit into friends,
as if the universe had been waiting
for their stories to collide,
for their hearts to find a home
in each other's presence.

We are connected,
not just at the hip,
but at the heart.
Best friends,
not by chance,
but by the kind of bond
that life itself couldn't break.

The way you feel is special,
not a curse,
even when it feels overwhelming.
You feel everything so deeply
because you care—
because your heart refuses
to stay at the surface.

Your depth is your strength,
a rare gift in a world
that too often shies away
from emotion.

Don't let anyone convince you
that caring too much is a flaw.
It's the bravest thing you can do—
to feel,
to care,
to love without limits.

My heart sings a happy song
because you care,
because you show up.

In a life where showing up for me
was rare,
where love felt distant,
you changed my world.
You made something shift,
made me believe
that I could be enough,
that I deserved this.

You make me feel valid,
happy,
loved in a way
I never thought I'd find.

You make me feel at home—
not just in a place,
but in myself.

MY LETTER:

Angelina Schreiber

MY LETTER:

_____

_____

_____

_____

_____

_____

_____

_____

_____

_____

_____

_____

_____

_____

_____

_____

_____

_____

_____

_____

_____

_____

_____

_____

_____

_____

_____

_____

_____

_____

to a friend
you've grown
apart from

There lives a villain in every story,
and sometimes, it's hard to tell who wears the mask.
But the most tragic story of all
is the one where I was yours.

I hope when you look into the mirror,
you see my reflection breaking and burning down.
I hope you see yourself break.
I hope you see yourself burn.

Sometimes,
I want to watch you from afar,
to see you chase your dreams,
to silently cheer you on,
as if my quiet support
could still reach you.

I want you to know
I still care,
even though life pulled us
onto separate paths,
even though we've grown
in different directions.

There's a part of me
that will always root for you,
a soft place in my heart
reserved for the memory of us.
No distance can erase that.

M Y L E T T E R :

Angelina Schreiber

M Y   L E T T E R :

We were speaking
the same language growing up,
and I never knew how to say sorry.

I changed myself
into a way I never wanted to.
I changed myself so much,
people started to look up to me.
People started to care.

Everyone except you.
You never loved me.
Neither the change.
And so, I am here.
Not myself anymore,
grieving for the time I was.

I was admiring you
with every breath I took,
with every step I took,
with every game you played.

I was admiring you with every vein
my heart was carrying.
I was admiring you.

And you. You were too. *Admiring yourself.*

I opened my soul to you,
each fragile piece laid bare,
offering you the parts of me
I rarely let anyone see.

But all you did was laugh—
at my cracks,
at my scars,
at the stories
that made me who I am.

Your laughter echoed,
sharp and hollow,
shattering the trust
I had placed in your hands.

MY LETTER:

_____

_____

_____

_____

_____

_____

_____

_____

_____

_____

_____

_____

_____

_____

_____

_____

_____

_____

_____

_____

_____

_____

_____

_____

_____

_____

_____

_____

_____

Angelina Schreiber

M Y L E T T E R :

Birthdays are hard when you've spent 23 years waiting for someone special to call, to remember you in a way that feels like you mattered to them. But the phone stays quiet, and you realize— it's just a normal day for them, while for you, it's a quiet ache, a reminder of all the ways you've hoped for more. Birthdays are hard, not because of the years passing, but because of the people who didn't show up when you needed them most.

I see you.
The world feels broken when, on a day meant for you,
everyone else takes the spotlight.
It's hard when you're lost in the noise,
when you just want to feel seen.

But know this:
You matter, even when it doesn't feel like it.
You deserve love and celebration,
and I hope you find a moment to remind yourself of that.

You are enough.

It wasn't about the gift.
It was about the thought,
the care,
the way it could've shown me
I mattered enough
to be celebrated.

It's the one day
you should feel special,
yet the silence screams louder
than any gift could.

And as the tears fall,
you realize:
sometimes, the hardest thing
is learning to be your own celebration,
to fill the emptiness
with the love
you deserve to give yourself.

MY LETTER:

_____

_____

_____

_____

_____

_____

_____

_____

_____

_____

_____

_____

_____

_____

_____

_____

_____

_____

_____

_____

_____

_____

_____

_____

_____

_____

_____

_____

_____

_____

_____

_____

Angelina Schreiber

M Y   L E T T E R :

to the person
you've never
forgiven

At least I don't have a heart condition, that's what they've said, Laughing, smoking, as if it's all in their head. They jest, but it's serious, this heart's silent song, It's the way we were made, fragile yet strong. Maybe they should stop smoking, it's more than a joke, each puff they take, another health spoke they broke. Joking's fine, but not when stakes are this high, start acting now, protect your heart before you sigh. For every beat is a gift, a delicate treasure, A rhythm that dances to life's precious measure. Take heed of the signs, and the lessons we learn, For once the heart falters, there's no easy return. It's not just a jest, but a mission we face, to care for our hearts, to keep up the pace. Spread the word, let the truth be known, in every heartbeat, our strength is shown. So cherish the gift, with every beat that resounds, For the heart is a guardian, where life truly grounds. Let's protect it with love, with actions so wise, for a healthy heart is where true happiness lies.

Do you teach them how to ride a bike,
steadying their handlebars, holding them close
until they're ready to let go?

Do you cheer them on,
step by step, in ways you never did with me?

Do you laugh with them, that easy,
unguarded kind of laughter
I used to wish was meant for me?

Do you make time, real time,
showing up for every moment that matters?
Are you the person now
that I once needed you to be?

Have you finally learned to love,
in the way I kept hoping for—
the way I waited for, but never got to see?

I am over you,
in every way possible.
I don't care about you.
I am just not over the fact
what you did to me, leaving scars.

You used words
that felt like they were wrapped in warmth,
words I thought were meant for love.

And you made me believe
that this was normal,
that this was real,
that maybe I deserved to hear them.

But now I wonder
if they were just words to you,
while I built a home
inside their meaning.

M Y L E T T E R :

Angelina Schreiber

M Y L E T T E R :

_____

_____

_____

_____

_____

_____

_____

_____

_____

_____

_____

_____

_____

_____

_____

_____

_____

_____

_____

_____

_____

_____

_____

_____

_____

_____

_____

_____

to your greatest fear

I am afraid to be left
with the weight of loneliness,
carrying the quiet ache
of not knowing what I did wrong—
what part of me wasn't enough
to make them stay.

Sometimes I am afraid
that they were right—
that I am hard to love,
hard to keep,
hard to cherish.

Their words linger,
etched into the quiet corners of my mind,
whispering doubts
that grow louder in the silence.

I wonder if there's something in me
too sharp, too heavy,
too much to hold.

The fear isn't in loving—
it's in not being able to share it,
in not being able to offer it
to the ones who need it,
to the ones who matter.

It's the thought of never finding
a way to show how much I care,
of never being able
to wrap my love in words,
or actions,
or the smallest gestures.

And in that fear,
I wonder—
will my love ever find its way out?
Will it ever be enough?

I healed, I really did.
But what if I'm still a cracked vase,
holding the flowers I never let go of—
beautiful, but not quite whole?

MY LETTER:

_____
_____
_____
_____
_____
_____
_____
_____
_____
_____
_____
_____
_____
_____
_____
_____
_____
_____
_____
_____
_____
_____
_____
_____
_____
_____
_____
_____
_____
_____
_____

Angelina Schreiber

M Y   L E T T E R :

I am sorry if at some point in life
I was an almost to you.
I know what it feels like.
To be enough, but not for them.
To fit, but not with them.
I am sorry if at some point in life
I was an almost to you.
You are enough. I promise.

I am sitting here,
writing poems straight from my mind,
since the night we talked for the first time—
words spilling out like they've always known you.

And you are out there,
treating everyone else the same,
like none of this matters,
like our conversations were just another passing moment.

Funny, isn't it?
How something so simple for you
has become everything to me.

Suddenly my favorite smell is Christmas trees.
Suddenly my favorite food is an avocado salad.
Suddenly my favorite animals are chameleons.
Suddenly my favorite thing to do is lay in the summer grass.
Suddenly my favorite movie is the grinch.

Suddenly my favorite color is green.

I hope I never want to write poetry about you— because poetry is where I go to grieve, where I pour the pieces of love that couldn't hold together. I hope I never have to carve you into lines meant to soothe an ache, never have to capture your memory in words meant to survive your absence. But if I do, if the day comes when you are no longer here, I know the poetry will find me anyway, and I will write of you— not because I want to, but because it's the only way to hold on to what's left.

M Y L E T T E R :

Angelina Schreiber

MY LETTER:

A Million Letters to Write

Spring arrives quietly,
whispering through the trees,
painting the sky in softer blues,
while the earth shakes off its winter coat.

The flowers stretch their petals,
like they've been waiting for this moment—
for the warmth to wrap around them
and remind them of who they are.

The air smells like possibility,
and each breath feels like renewal,
like the world is starting over,
inviting us to do the same.

In spring, we're reminded
that even after the coldest of winters,
growth finds a way,
and life always comes back.

In its embrace,
the world feels both wild and free—
a fleeting season,
but a memory that lasts forever.

The trees let go of their leaves,
letting them dance in the wind,
as if saying goodbye with grace,
knowing that letting go
is a part of growing.

The trees stand bare,
their branches etched against a gray sky,
but there's a certain stillness in their bones,
as if they too are waiting for something new.

The cold sharpens the world,
making every moment feel sharper,
clearer,
as the nights grow long and quiet.

But in winter, there is warmth,
found in the flicker of a fire,
in the comfort of familiar spaces,
in the tenderness of shared moments.

It's a season of slowing down,
of reflecting,
of finding beauty in the starkness,
and remembering that even in the coldest of times,
there is peace in the waiting.

M Y   L E T T E R :

_____

_____

_____

_____

_____

_____

_____

_____

_____

_____

_____

_____

_____

_____

_____

_____

_____

_____

_____

_____

_____

_____

_____

_____

_____

_____

_____

_____

Angelina Schreiber

M Y L E T T E R :

Our eyes meet,
a silent understanding passing between them,
a knowing far deeper than words.

They realize what is about to happen—
the shift, the fall, the inevitability.
They knew far earlier
than our hearts ever did,
as if they saw the ending
before we even began.

In that moment,
it feels like everything pauses,
like the world is holding its breath,
waiting for us to catch up
to what our eyes already knew.

The moment I stepped onto this stage,
I felt it—
a rush of pride,
not just for being here,
but for every step it took to get here.

Every stumble, every triumph,
every moment that shaped me,
led me to this place.

And standing here,
I finally felt it in my bones:
this is where I belong.
This is the space I've been chasing,
the one I was meant to fill all along.

In your arms for the first time,
felt like a storm finally quieting,
like finding shore after being lost at sea.

The Christmas tree
sparkled with a thousand lights,
each one casting a glow
that seemed to wrap around us,
but in that moment,
the presents under the tree didn't matter.

What mattered was the way
we all fit together,
like pieces of a puzzle
that had found their place.

M Y   L E T T E R :

Angelina Schreiber

MY LETTER:

A Million Letters to Write

What are the odds,
that we live in the same universe
where Icarus flew too high,
his wings made of hope and wax,
his heart burning for something more?

What are the odds that our love
echoes their story—
two souls reaching for the sun,
knowing the danger,
yet unwilling to stop?

Maybe we're not so different from Icarus,
chasing something just out of reach,
flying too close to a dream
that may burn us in the end.

But what are the odds,
that in the vastness of the universe,
our hearts found each other anyway?
Maybe that's the beauty of it—
in the grand story,
even the fallen ones are remembered.

He made her change.
Because of him,
she could never stop looking for the sun,
because it makes her think about him.

Today I saw the sun smile again.
It was the smile you get
when the darkest rain leaves.
Even though it doesn't want to.

It was the smile you get
after the scariest night is over.

The smile you get
when it is just by itself.
Lingering in warmth and hope
it smiled its breathtaking smile.

Today I saw your smile, and I swear
it looked like the sun finally rose again.

She's always been the center,
the force that holds everything together,
but sometimes, she forgets
that she too can sparkle
in ways only the darkness can reveal.

She shines in her own way,
even if she's yet to see
how magnificent her light is.

MY LETTER:

Angelina Schreiber

M Y   L E T T E R :

Being the one in the family that writes is a gift.
Because on every beautiful occasion
like a wedding or a birthday,
you let the words dance across the room
and let everybody there feel your emotions.

But it's also a curse.
Because with your words
you and everyone in your family
says goodbye to people
you would like to spend every word
on *begging them to stay.*

And I asked myself, what would be the first thing you two would do together. Maybe you would tell him everything that happened to us, to your family. And he would tell you everything he saw from heaven. Maybe you would laugh, maybe you would cry. But deep down I know, in heaven you two would dance again. Finally.

In a room full of people, I've ever met,
I would look for my grandpa
and tell him that I made it.
Longer than I thought I would.
I would hug him once more.

Dear grandpa E.
& dear grandpa W.
& dear grandma I.

The universe gained
another three stars
with your absence on earth.

You will never be forgotten.

M Y   L E T T E R :

Angelina Schreiber

M Y L E T T E R :

She thought she wouldn't make it alone
but the only person that ever hold her hand
crying was herself.
So, she knew that she will be fine.

For so long, I searched for who I was,
but now, I see her clearly
in the ripples of the water,
in the way the sun dances on the surface,
gentle and radiant.

I no longer see just the surface,
but the depth beneath it—
a collection of dreams,
of laughter,
of scars turned into stories.

I'm not perfect,
but I am whole,
and the reflection staring back at me
is the one I've been waiting for all along.

Why is the person in the mirror
always the one we hate the most,
when it's the one we should cherish forever?

We see the mistakes,
the things we wish we could change,
but we forget that the person in the mirror
is the only one who has truly stayed with us,
through every storm,
through every joy.

The mirror saw us in every form,
from the days we were small,
uncertain,
to the moments we stood tall,
with shoulders back and hearts open.

It witnessed our tears,
the times we crumbled,
and the times we rose,
stronger than before.

Through every change,
every version of ourselves,
the mirror never turned away—
it just reflected who we were,
who we are,
and who we're becoming.

In its silent stillness,
the mirror holds our truth,
a reminder that we've always been
everything we need to be,
even when we didn't see it ourselves.

M Y   L E T T E R :

Angelina Schreiber

MY LETTER:

In five years,
you will ache
to hug the person
you see in the mirror right now,
so don't hesitate.

You don't need someone
to tell you they're proud.

Being proud of yourself is enough.

I hope in 10 years,
I will look back and find myself,
not just in the places I've been,
but in the way I've grown,
in the peace I've built,
in the love I've given and received.

I hope I'll be able to smile,
knowing that no matter where life took me,
I found my way back to the one place
that has always been mine—
a home,
not in a house,
but in my heart.

The stars may shift,
the paths may twist,
but I believe that destiny will unfold,
and in the end,
I'll be right where I'm meant to be—
surrounded by the love and life
I was always meant to find.

MY LETTER:

Angelina Schreiber

M Y L E T T E R :

A Million Letters to Write

What if the books on your bedside table are telling the story you could have if you start living life as an opportunity. Because this is what life simply is — an opportunity. An opportunity of becoming who you really want to be and mostly an opportunity of doing the things your heart aches for. It is your opportunity of creating yourself the way an author creates their characters — with flaws and hope. Giving them every opportunity to grow.

In a world full of unwritten books,
be the one an author is inspired
to write day and night.

Be the one that shocks everyone.
Be the one nobody can put back into the shelf.

You are a masterpiece,
no matter what they say,
no matter how loud they laugh.

You painted yourself
with the colors of resilience,
with strokes of courage and grace.
Every shade, every line,
is exactly as it was meant to be—
a reflection of the soul
only you can see.

You are art,
raw and breathtaking,
and you've always had the right
to create yourself
exactly as you are.

MY LETTER:

Angelina Schreiber

M Y   L E T T E R :

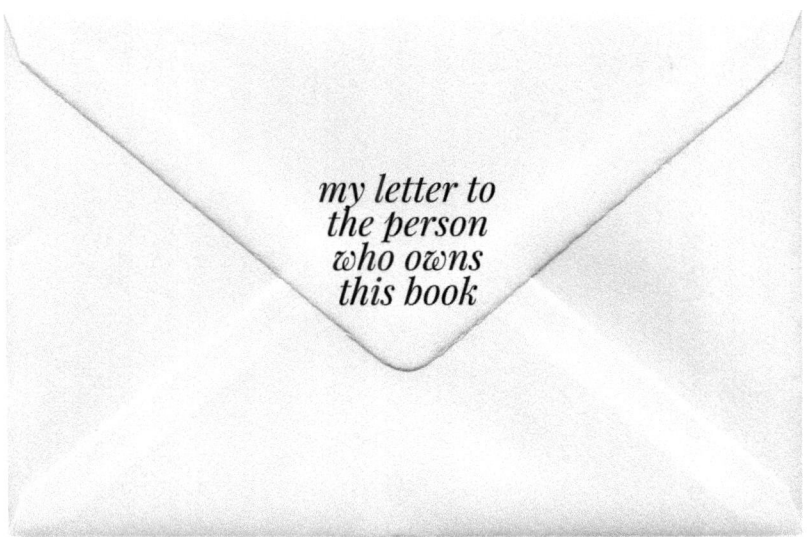

Dear Reader,

Thank you for reading and writing with me,
for letting my words find their way into your heart.
Thank you for your million thoughts and letters,
for the quiet moments we've shared
even from a distance.

Every word written was for you,
to remind you that emotions are never too much,
that your feelings are valid,
and that you are seen,
even when the world feels blind to your light.

And when you come back to these poems and letters—
whether in joy or sadness—
I hope you feel the warmth of these pages,
like a friend sitting beside you in the silence.

Remember this: you are never alone.
These words will hold you
when no one else can,
a steady hand reaching out to remind you
that you are always enough,
and you are always loved.

With all my heart,
Angelina

A Million Letters to Write

Angelina Schreiber

More books by Angelina Schreiber

My State of Felicity

dear inner child

More of Angelina's work

@poetrybyangii

A Million Letters to Write